CARTOONING FOR BEGINNERS

A STEP BY STEP GUIDE TO DRAWING CARTOONS

by ·MADDOCKS·

 MICHAEL O'MARA BOOKS LIMITED

FIRST PUBLISHED IN 1992 IN GREAT BRITAIN BY
MICHAEL O'MARA BOOKS LIMITED, 9 LION YARD
TREMADOC ROAD, LONDON. SW4 7NQ.

COPYRIGHT © 1992 BY PETER MADDOCKS

A CIP CATALOGUE RECORD FOR THIS BOOK IS
AVAILABLE FROM THE BRITISH LIBRARY.

ISBN 1-85479-161-3

PRINTED AND BOUND IN PORTUGAL BY
PRINTER PORTUGUESA.

TAKE A GOOD LOOK THROUGH THE BOOK
FIRST BEFORE YOU START TO DRAW—
THEN, WHEN YOU FEEL INSPIRED START
WORK WITH YOUR PEN AND ENJOY
YOURSELF... THERE'S LOTS OF THINGS
TO COPY OR TRACE TO GIVE YOU AN IDEA
OF HOW TO PUT A CHARACTER OR A
CARTOON TOGETHER.
DON'T FORGET THAT PRACTICE MAKES
PERFECT SO IF YOU DON'T GET IT RIGHT
FIRST TIME—DO IT AGAIN—AND
AGAIN!

DON'T BE AFRAID
TO COPY —
THAT'S HOW YOU
WILL LEARN...

OR TRACE — THIS WILL GIVE YOU
MORE CONFIDENCE IN YOUR LINE
DRAWING...

By Leigh

AFTER WATCHING THE OLD MOVIE CALLED 'MOBY DICK'
MY SIX YEAR OLD GRANDSON DID THE ABOVE DRAWING.
VERY BASIC, VERY SIMPLE, YET ALL THE STORY TELLING
INGREDIENTS ARE THERE — CAPTAIN AHAB TELLING
HIS CREW TO CHASE THE GREAT WHITE WHALE WITH
THEIR HARPOONS... A GOOD ILLUSTRATION.

IF YOU DRAW LIKE THIS—DON'T WORRY

IT'S NOT TOO FAR AWAY FROM DRAWING LIKE THIS...

JUST FOLLOW THIS BOOK FROM PAGE TO PAGE WITH PENCIL, PAPER AND PEN AND I'LL HAVE YOU DRAWING LIKE A CARTOONIST IN NO TIME...

TAKE YOUR TIME AND ENJOY YOUR DRAWING —
DON'T MAKE HARD WORK OF IT, DRAWING CARTOONS IS

FUN!

NOTTHING

BUT THERE ARE CERTAIN RULES TO FOLLOW...

EVERYTHING IN THIS BOOK—AND THAT INCLUDES THE LETTERING—IS DRAWN WITH A FIBRE TIP PEN

HOWEVER...

EVEN IF THE BLACK FIBRE-TIP PEN IS CLEANER AND EASIER TO USE—

DON'T LET ME PUT YOU OFF USING A DIP PEN AND BLACK INDIAN INK— IT IS A BEAUTIFUL WAY TO DRAW EVEN IF YOU DO GET BLOBS, BLOTS AND INKY FINGERS...

THE FIRST THING YOU WILL NEED IS AN HB PENCIL

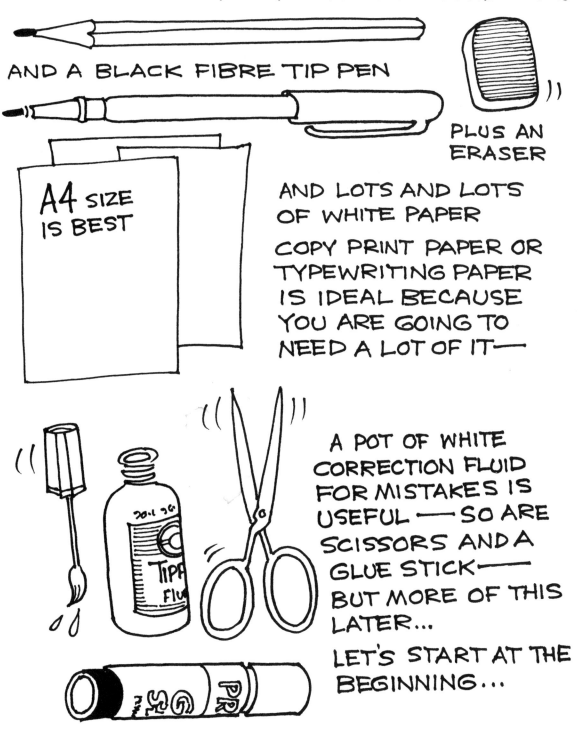

AND A BLACK FIBRE TIP PEN

PLUS AN ERASER

A4 SIZE IS BEST

AND LOTS AND LOTS OF WHITE PAPER

COPY PRINT PAPER OR TYPEWRITING PAPER IS IDEAL BECAUSE YOU ARE GOING TO NEED A LOT OF IT—

A POT OF WHITE CORRECTION FLUID FOR MISTAKES IS USEFUL — SO ARE SCISSORS AND A GLUE STICK— BUT MORE OF THIS LATER...

LET'S START AT THE BEGINNING...

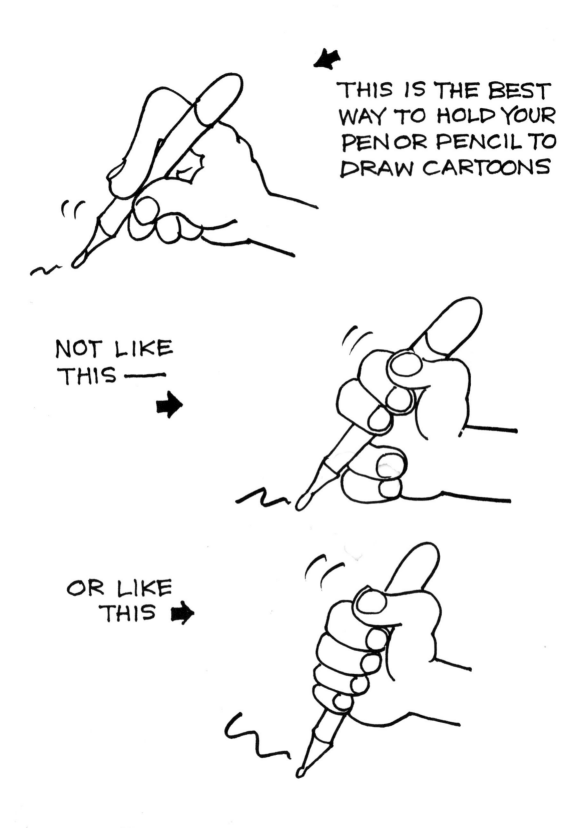

THIS IS THE BEST
WAY TO HOLD YOUR
PEN OR PENCIL TO
DRAW CARTOONS

NOT LIKE
THIS —

OR LIKE
THIS

WE START WITH HOW TO DRAW A CARTOON
FACE — START WITH A CIRCLE, USE A
COMPASS OR DRAW FREEHAND WITH A PEN...

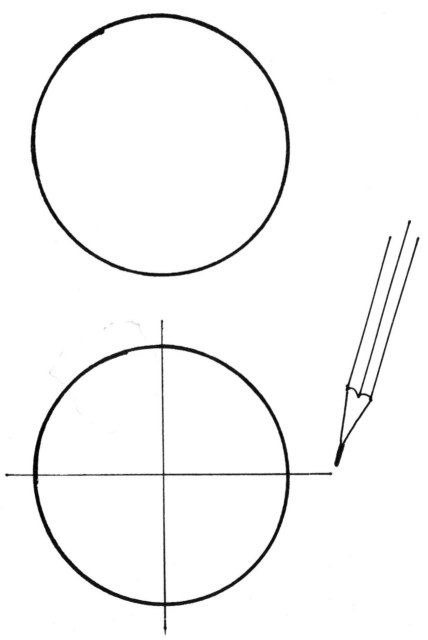

THEN WITH A PENCIL — DRAW A **CROSS**

USE A FIBRE TIP PEN TO DRAW A CIRCLE

USE A PENCIL TO MAKE A CROSS

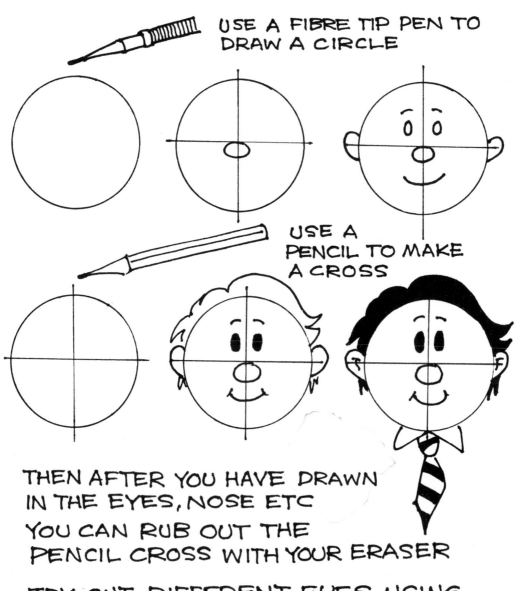

THEN AFTER YOU HAVE DRAWN IN THE EYES, NOSE ETC

YOU CAN RUB OUT THE PENCIL CROSS WITH YOUR ERASER

TRY OUT DIFFERENT EYES USING BLACK DOTS OR JUST CIRCLES

OR DOTS INSIDE THE CIRCLES

TRY OUT FACES WITH SMILING MOUTHS OR MOUTH SHOWING TEETH ...

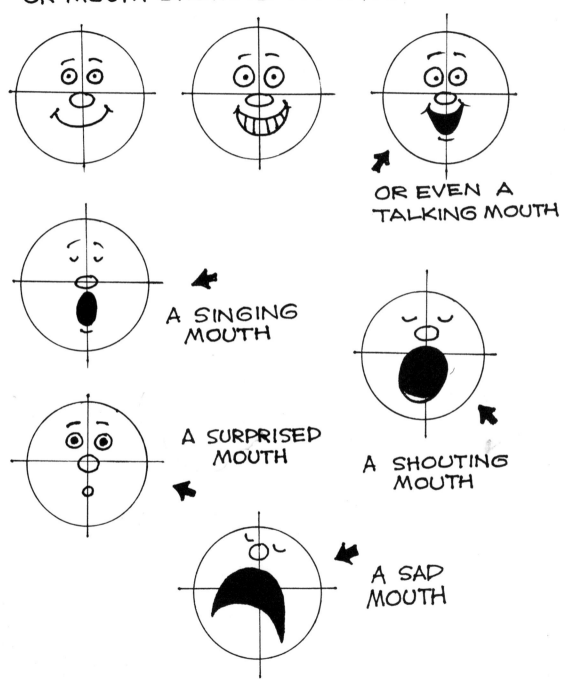

OR EVEN A TALKING MOUTH

A SINGING MOUTH

A SURPRISED MOUTH

A SHOUTING MOUTH

A SAD MOUTH

JUST DRAW LOTS OF CIRCLES AND EXPERIMENT

NOW HAVE A GO AT DRAWING DIFFERENT HAIRLINES — DRAW LOTS OF CIRCLES...

LEAVE SOME OPEN...

BLACK SOME IN...

TRY BALD HEADS...

SPIKEY HAIR...

OR SAILOR'S HAT

IT'S GREAT FUN — HAVE A GO...

NOW TRY
SOME GIRLS'
FACES WITH
RIBBONS
CURLS
AND HATS

LOTS OF
EXPRESSIONS!
HAPPY AND
SAD

TO MOVE THE HEAD AROUND TRY TO
IMAGINE YOU ARE DRAWING A FOOTBALL

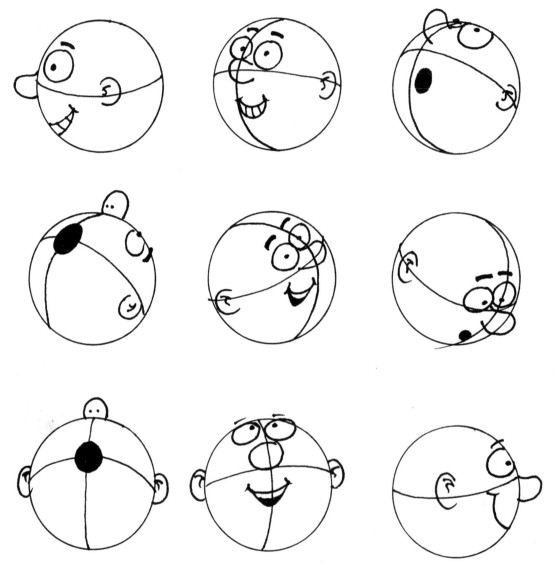

PENCIL IN THE CURVES AND DRAW
YOUR FACES — THIS EXERCISE IS A
LITTLE DIFFICULT, BUT PRACTICE WILL
MAKE PERFECT — RUB OUT THE PENCIL
LINES LATER...

KEEP THE FEATURES SIMPLE—

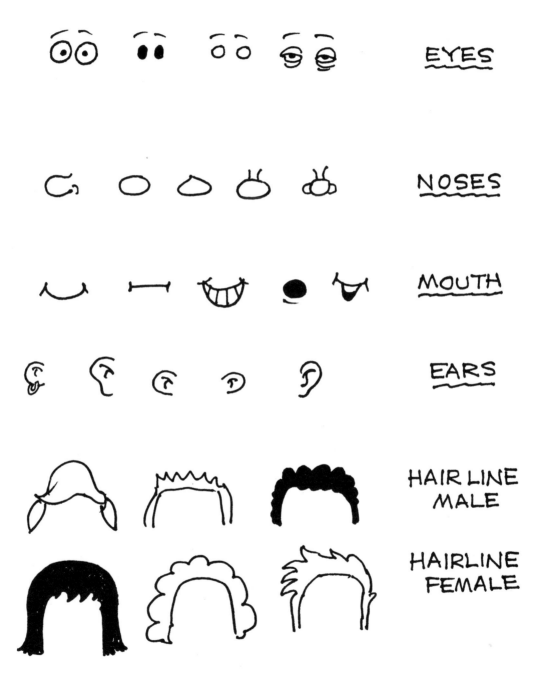

EYES

NOSES

MOUTH

EARS

HAIR LINE
MALE

HAIRLINE
FEMALE

AFTER A WHILE YOU WILL STOP DRAWING
CIRCLES FOR A FACE AND DRAW IT
FREEHAND... AS YOU GET USED TO IT —

YOU WILL THEN
DRAW YOUR
CHARACTER QUITE
NATURALLY...

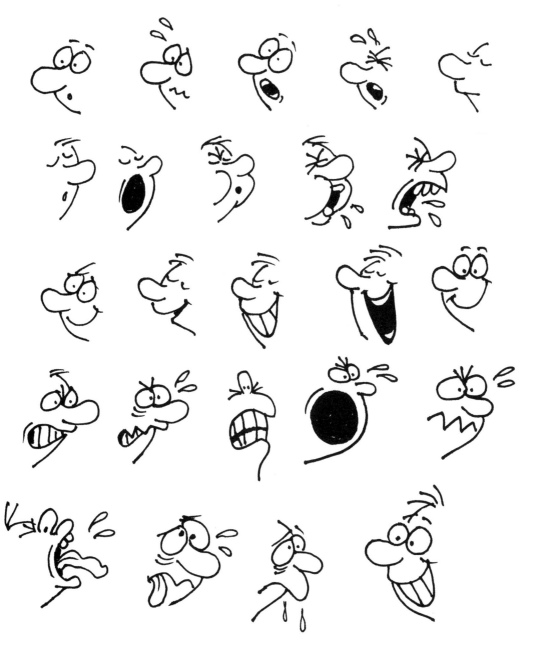

LOOK IN THE MIRROR AND PULL FACES —
THEN JOT THEM DOWN ON PAPER YUK!

FACES — OR I SHOULD SAY — PULLING FACES...

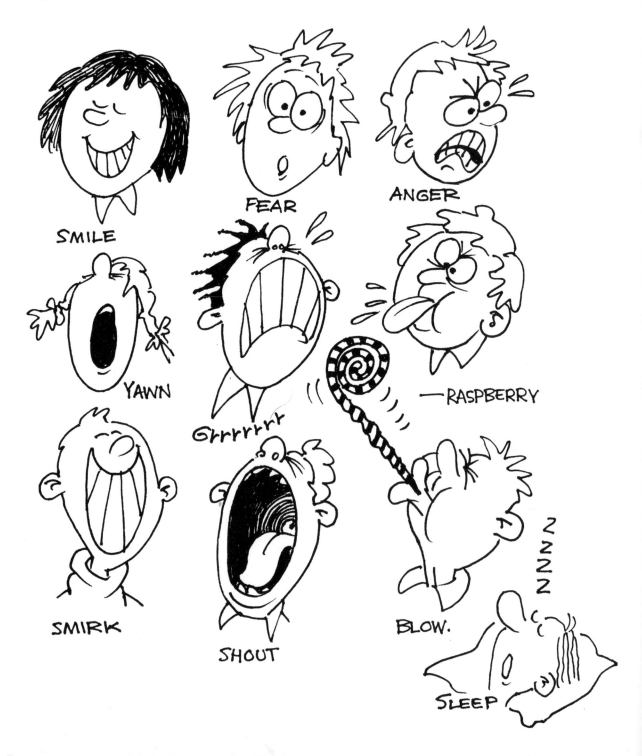

SMILE

FEAR

ANGER

YAWN

Grrrrrrr

RASPBERRY

SMIRK

SHOUT

BLOW.

ZZZZ

SLEEP

EXPRESSIONS...

 SMILE...

 POO!

 HMMM...

 WAAAGH!

 OOPS! OH DEAR...

 GRRRR!

 YOW! HELP!

 OH WELL!

 HAR! HE HEE

 HAW!

MORE FACES...

KEEP DRAWING EXPRESSIONS — YOU CAN
ALWAYS INVENT A NEW ONE, A YAWN, A COUGH,
A SCREAM... ALL USEFUL CARTOON FACES...

DRAWING HANDS —

KEEP THEM SIMPLE...

PALMS OPEN...
THUMBS OUT

PALMS CLOSED
THUMBS IN

HAND WITH NAILS

BABY
HAND

GIRL'S
HAND

BOY'S
HAND

BUNCH OF
FIVES!

YUK!

OH LOOK!

HANDS TOGETHER

DON'T BOTHER WITH FINGERNAILS AND
KNUCKLE CREASES — IT COMPLICATES
THE DRAWING OF HANDS...

KEEP THE DRAWING OPEN
AND SIMPLE...

THEY ARE VERY IMPORTANT
SO KEEP DRAWING HANDS — THERE'S LOTS
OF EXPRESSION
IN HANDS...

FEET—

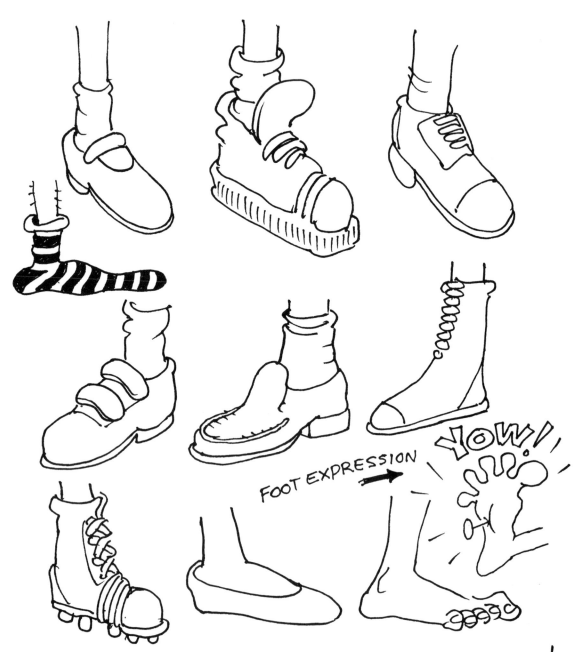

FOOT EXPRESSION →

YOW!

NOT MUCH YOU CAN SAY ABOUT FEET!
BUT WATCH THE CHANGING FASHIONS IN SHOES

DRAWING A FAMILY

ON THE FOLLOWING PAGES YOU WILL SEE
I HAVE DRAWN A FAMILY GROUP FOR YOU TO
PRACTISE YOUR FACES AND EXPRESSIONS.

MUM

JANE

DAD

JIMMY

THE FAMILY CONSISTS OF MUM, DAD, JANE,
JIMMY, JORDAN, LUCY, SPORRAN THE DOG
AND MAX THE CAT...

YOU WILL FIND THAT YOU WILL BE ABLE TO
ADD ALL KINDS OF EXPRESSIONS INTO THE
BLANK FACES THAT FOLLOW—THIS SHOULD
HELP YOU TO GET USED TO PULLING FACES
WITHOUT HAVING TO DRAW THE COMPLETE
HEAD EVERY TIME...

JORDAN

SPORRAN

LUCY

MAX

MUM

TRACE
THE FACE
OUTLINES...

OR IF MUM OR
DAD'S GOT A
COPY PRINT
MACHINE —

DAD

GET THEM TO
RUN A FEW
COPIES OFF
FOR YOU TO
PRACTISE ON

EITHER WAY
TRY DRAWING
IN THE FACES
WITH YOUR
FIBRE TIP
PEN...

JANE

JIMMY

JORDAN

Robert

Robert

Reld

Dog

Cate

Car

House

LUCY

SPORRAN

MAX

THIS IS A DRAWING FROM A PHOTOGRAPH OF A SCHOOLBOY I SAW IN A NEWSPAPER...

THIS IS A CARTOON DRAWING OF THE SAME BOY

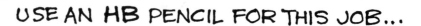

USE AN **HB** PENCIL FOR THIS JOB...

FIRST DRAW A SIMPLE
LITTLE MAN SHAPE LIKE
THIS...

DRAW HIM IN PENCIL
LOTS OF TIMES UNTIL
YOU GET USED TO
HIS SIZE — DON'T
MAKE HIS HEAD
TOO BIG OR TOO
SMALL...

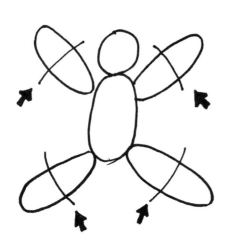

THEN THINK ABOUT THE ELBOW JOINTS AND
THE KNEE JOINTS — THEY BEND HALF
WAY UP THE ARMS AND HALF WAY UP THE
LEGS, REMEMBER THIS WHEN YOUR LITTLE
MAN SITS DOWN...

WHEN YOU GET USED TO GETTING SOME MOVEMENT INTO YOUR CHARACTER, TRY ADDING HANDS AND FEET — KEEP THEM SIMPLE — NO FINGERNAILS OR LACES YET...

PALMS UP — THUMBS OUT

PALMS DOWN — THUMBS IN

WHEN YOU CAN DRAW YOUR LITTLE MAN WITH HIS HANDS AND FEET TRY ADDING SOME CLOTHES LIKE A JACKET COLLAR AND TIE...

TRY SEPARATING THE HAND FROM THE SLEEVE BY ADDING A WHITE CUFF

THEN BLACK IN THE JACKET WITH YOUR PEN OR BRUSH

A STRIPED TIE

OR JUST GIVE HIM A SWEATER AND JEANS

NO — I HAVEN'T FORGOTTEN THE GIRLS —
YOU'LL NEED TO SHARPEN YOUR PENCIL AND
PAY A LITTLE MORE ATTENTION WHEN
DRAWING THE FEMALE OF THE SPECIES...

GIRLS ARE MUCH PRETTIER
THAN MEN SO THEY ARE MORE
DIFFICULT TO DRAW — YOU
HAVE TO GET THEIR LEGS RIGHT

YOU WILL ALSO FIND THAT WHEN
YOU DO GET THE LEGS RIGHT —
SHE'S ABOUT SIX FEET TALL

THEY MOVE DIFFERENTLY FROM MEN — WATCH HOW
SHE WALKS, STANDS AND SITS DOWN...

A BIT MORE
STYLE—

A LOT MORE
GRACE...

AND YOU DON'T HAVE TO
GIVE THEM LARGE BUSTS...

UNLESS OF COURSE YOU ARE DRAWING PEOPLE LIKE THIS!

THEN OF COURSE BIG CHESTS
AND FAT TUMS ARE PART
OF THE CHARACTER—

THAT ALSO
INCLUDES
BIG BUMS!

SIZES: DRAW AN ADULT 4 HEADS HIGH
DRAW A CHILD 3 HEADS HIGH
A BABY IS ONLY 2 HEADS HIGH

BIG GEORGE
IS ABOUT 4
HEADS HIGH

LITTLE GEORGE
IS ABOUT 3
HEADS HIGH

A BABY IS
2 HEADS HIGH

DRAWING A BABY...

DRAW A BABY ABOUT TWO HEADS HIGH — THE SAME AS YOU WOULD DRAW A CAT...

AND REMEMBER THAT BABIES PULL A LOT OF FUNNY FACES —

TAKE YOUR STICK MAN...

GIVE HIM HANDS AND SHOES AND TRY
MOVING HIM AROUND — THEN GIVE HIM A
TRACK SUIT — AND THEN FINALLY, A FACE

* START IN PENCIL — THEN INK HIM IN!

THIS IS GEORGE — TRY DRAWING HIM IN DIFFERENT POSITIONS

FROM THE FRONT...

FROM THE SIDE...

FROM THE BACK

FROM THE TOP

(IF YOU'RE A BIRD)

FROM THE GROUND (IF YOU'RE A WORM)

GOOD OLD GEORGE...

GEORGE IS WALKING...

UP STEPS...

DOWN STEPS...

CRAWLING UNDER COVERS...

IF YOU ARE NOT SURE HOW TO DRAW THE ACTIONS—STAND UP AND DO THEM, IT'S THE ONLY WAY TO FIND OUT.

THIS IS SUSIE, START BY DRAWING 3 CIRCLES

PIN WOMAN

WALKING

BACK VIEW

FRONT

SITTING

3 CIRCLES

1

2

3

THIS IS LITTLE SUSIE — DRAW HER WITH 2 CIRCLES

WALKING   FRONT   RUNNING

BACK VIEW   SITTING

LITTLE SUSIE'S
BABY SISTER

ACTION SKETCHES...

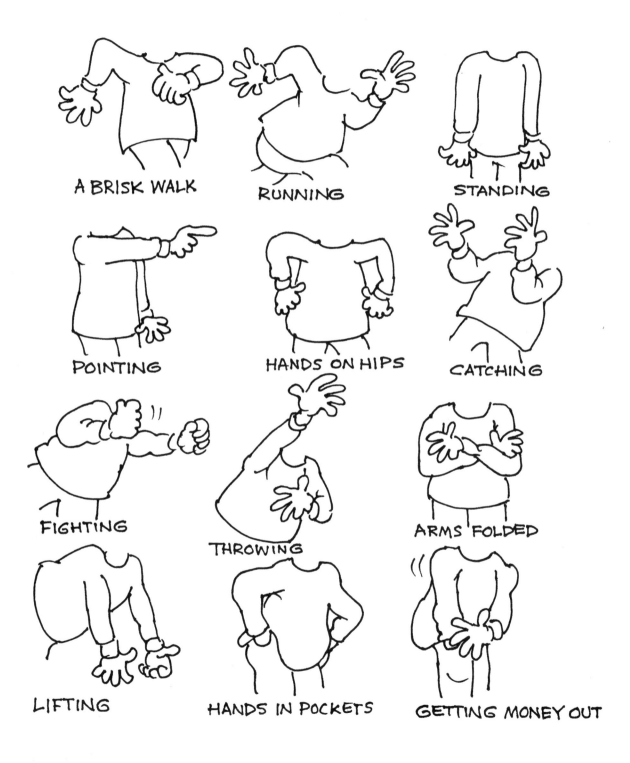

A BRISK WALK

RUNNING

STANDING

POINTING

HANDS ON HIPS

CATCHING

FIGHTING

THROWING

ARMS FOLDED

LIFTING

HANDS IN POCKETS

GETTING MONEY OUT

ACTION SKETCHES...

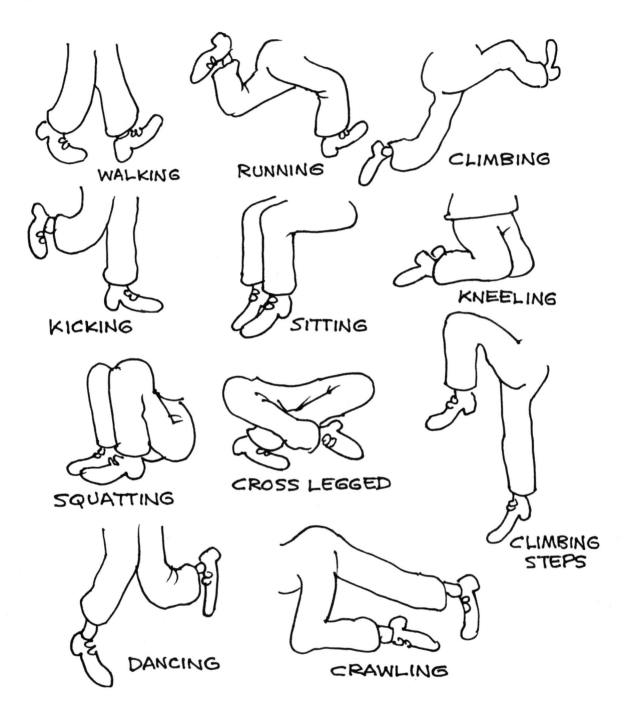

WALKING

RUNNING

CLIMBING

KICKING

SITTING

KNEELING

SQUATTING

CROSS LEGGED

CLIMBING STEPS

DANCING

CRAWLING

ACTION SKETCHES...

WALKING

RUNNING

CLIMBING

SITTING

STANDING

KNEELING

DANCING

CHASING BOYS

ACTION SKETCHES...

WORKING   THINKING   DESPERATE

GOT THE ANSWER   NOT SURE...   YES—I WAS RIGHT!

READING   SCRATCHING   RESTING

ACTION SKETCHES...

WALKING

RUNNING

STANDING

CLIMBING

SWINGING

KICKING

KNEELING

ACTION SKETCHES...

TALKING

SHOUTING

DESCRIBING

CARRYING

DRESSING

WASHING

BRUSHING

THINKING

IRONING

PUSHING

ACTION SKETCHES...

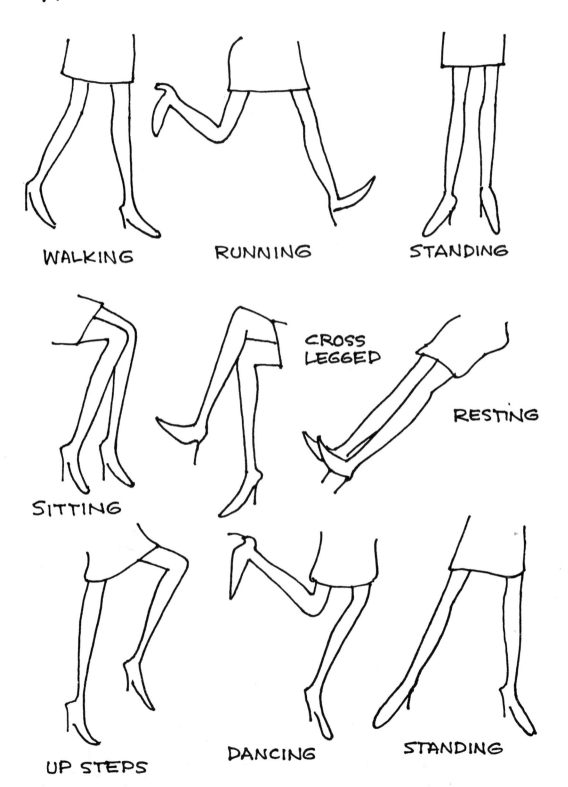

WALKING

RUNNING

STANDING

CROSS LEGGED

RESTING

SITTING

UP STEPS

DANCING

STANDING

I KNOW THAT BURGLARS DON'T REALLY
DRESS LIKE THIS

BUT IF YOU DRAW A CHARACTER LIKE THIS
EVERYBODY WHO SEE'S IT KNOWS EXACTLY
WHAT HIS NASTY BUSINESS IS —

SO UNTIL SOMEBODY CREATES ANOTHER
INSTANTLY RECOGNISABLE UNIFORM —
WHY CHANGE IT?

STEREOTYPES — WELL LOVED UNIFORMS...

MAKE SKETCHES OF PEOPLE IN UNIFORMS
YOU USE THEM A LOT IN CARTOONS...

SCHOOLBOY CHARACTERS!

SCHOOLGIRL CHARACTERS!

DRAWING SANTA...

DON'T FORGET—YOU
CAN ALWAYS DRAW YOUR
OWN CHRISTMAS CARDS
JUST ADD COLOUR...

OR ONE FOR YOUR BEST FRIEND

OR A **GET WELL SOON** CARD

TO YOUR <u>SECOND</u> BEST FRIEND!

WHEN YOU CAN DRAW CARTOONS YOU
CAN BRIGHTEN *ANYBODY'S* DAY!

ACTION—PLUS EXPRESSION...

THINK ABOUT THE ACTION BEFORE YOU DRAW IT — THIS GOALKEEPER HAS JUST LET IN AN EASY GOAL — SO HE'S NOT PLEASED. LET HIS EXPRESSION TELL A STORY...

EXPRESSION IS
EVERYTHING IN
CARTOONING—

THIS BOY IS
RUNNING BECAUSE
HE IS LATE FOR
SCHOOL...

WHERE AS—
THIS BOY IS
RUNNING TO
CATCH THE
ICE CREAM
VAN AFTER
SCHOOL

— SEE THE DIFFERENCE!

ACTION — PLUS EXPRESSION...

THIS BOY HAS JUST SEEN
THE SCHOOL BULLY HEADING
HIS WAY...

THE PUNCH —

BOP!

THINK ABOUT MOVEMENT — STAND IN FRONT
OF A MIRROR AND WATCH YOURSELF MOVE

USE YOUR PENCIL
TO DRAW STICK PEOPLE

GET THE FEELING OF
THE ACTION FIRST WITH
YOUR PENCIL — THEN
DRAW YOUR CHARACTER
WITH YOUR PEN ONCE YOU
ARE SURE OF THE POSITION
OF THE ARMS AND LEGS...

MOVEMENT... A VITAL PART OF CARTOONING...

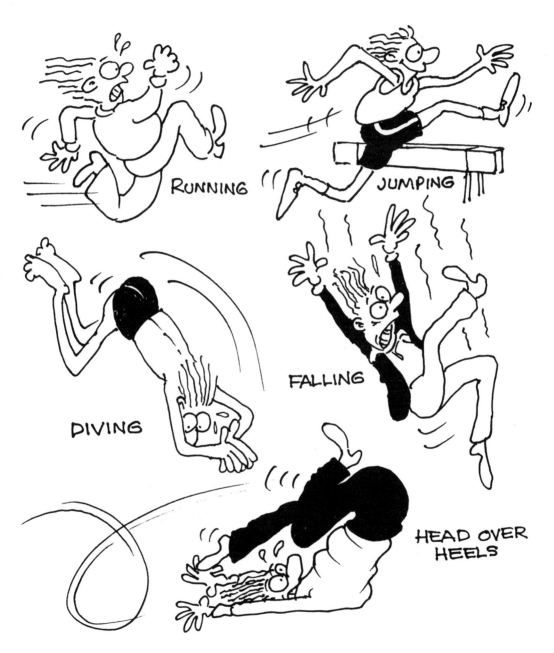

RUNNING

JUMPING

DIVING

FALLING

HEAD OVER HEELS

EXAGGERATE ALL MOVEMENT WITH SPEED LINES AND SWEAT MARKS...

WHAT IS A CARTOON?

TO GIVE AN EXAMPLE—
A CARTOON SITUATION
WHERE A MAN SLIPS
ON A BANANA SKIN...

CAN BE MADE FUNNIER
IF THE SAME MAN SLIPS
ON A BANANA SKIN—
CARRYING A DOZEN EGGS...

SKID!

EGGS EGGS

THE READER CAN THEN
IMAGINE WHAT WILL
HAPPEN NEXT——

SKID!

EVEN IF YOU DON'T DRAW IT.'

BUT IF YOU DO—IT WILL LOOK FUNNIER
THAN JUST A MAN SLIPPING ON A BANANA SKIN...

THAT IS A CARTOON!

← JUST DRAWING
TWO PEOPLE TALKING
TO EACH OTHER CAN
LOOK QUITE BORING

PUTTING THEM
IN A SITUATION
(LIKE SHOPPING
IN A SUPERMARKET)
CAN MAKE IT
LOOK MORE
INTERESTING.

THIS IS A DRAWING OF A MAN TALKING TO A BANK MANAGER — BUT IF YOU WANT YOUR PICTURE TO TELL A STORY...

THE DRAWING BELOW TELLS YOU WHY THE MAN IS TALKING TO A BANK MANAGER — MAKE YOUR PICTURE TELL THE STORY — AND YOUR CAPTION TELL THE GAG!

THIS IS A CARTOON DRAWING OF A MAN
WATCHING TELEVISION — KEEP THE
BACKGROUND SIMPLE — A DOORWAY,
A PICTURE ON THE WALL, A CAT, A CURTAIN,
A CUP OF TEA ON A TABLE AND THE
OUTLINE OF A RUG ON THE FLOOR...
THEN JUST BLACK IN THE TELEVISION IN
THE FOREGROUND...

KEEP THE BACKGROUND DETAIL SIMPLE —
BUT IT MUST TELL A STORY SO THAT THE
READER CAN IMMEDIATELY IDENTIFY
THE SITUATION...
NO NEED FOR VASTS AMOUNT OF DETAIL
JUST OUTLINES WILL DO...

NAMES ON A DOOR ARE USEFUL...

YOUR DRAWING MUST TELL A STORY— THEN WHATEVER THE GAG CAPTION IS TELLS THE JOKE — BUT YOUR READER MUST BE ABLE TO IDENTIFY THE SITUATION AT A GLANCE — THAT'S CARTOON DRAWING!

JOKES

JOKES

HAVE YOU EVER READ THE HEALTH
WARNING ON THE PACKET?

IT'S THE MAN IN THE IRON MASK!

WHAT IS A CARTOON?

THIS IS A PICTURE OF A MAN WITH A SIGN UNDER HIS ARM LOOKING DOWN A HOLE...

— NOT REALLY A CARTOON!

BUT IF YOU DRAW THE SAME SITUATION WITH
AN ANGRY BATTERED MAN CLIMBING BACK UP
OUT OF THE OTHER HOLE BEHIND THE MAN
WITH THE SIGN ——— THAT'S A CARTOON!

TAKE A DIVE IN THE SIXTH!

COME ON IN — HAVE YOU EATEN?

JOKES

JOKES

IS THIS YOUR CAR, SIR?

DRAWING ANIMALS...

DRAW THREE CIRCLES AND A SQUIGGLE LIKE THIS ➤

THEN ADD TWO DOTS FOR EYES

THIS FACE WILL PROVIDE YOU WITH AN EXPRESSION FOR LOTS OF ANIMALS

LIKE A CAT ➤

OR A DOG ➤

◄ OR EVEN A SEALION —

SAME FACE!

MAKE GOOD USE OF YOUR
LOCAL ZOO—

SKETCH THE
ANIMALS...

☆
START A
REFERENCE BOOK
FILL IT WITH DRAWINGS OF ANIMALS...

ADD A FROWN

AND THE SAME
FACE CAN BE A
FEROCIOUS LION...

OR A TIGER...

OR EVEN A CUB

YOU CAN
ALSO ADD
TEETH Grrrrrr

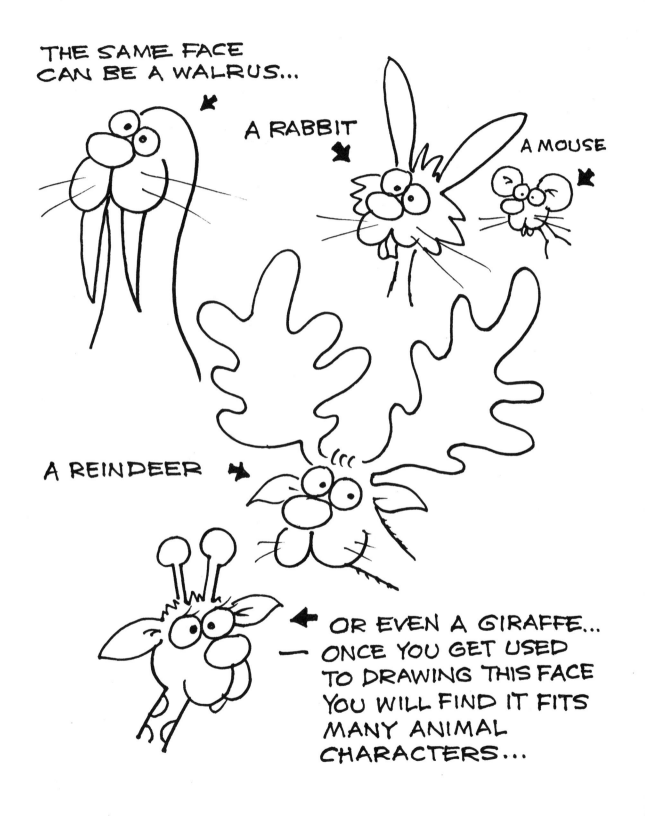

THINK ABOUT THE ANIMAL
YOU ARE GOING TO DRAW—

HOW DOES IT STAND?
HOW DOES IT MOVE?
HOW DOES IT SIT?

GET TO KNOW
ITS SHAPE!

THINK OF THE SHAPE
OF THE ANIMAL FIRST

THEN PENCIL
THE OUTLINE OF
THE ANIMAL YOU
HAVE IN MIND

THIS WILL HELP
YOU TO UNDERSTAND
YOUR CHARACTER
MORE —

FIT THE
EXPRESSIONS
TO THE
ACTION!

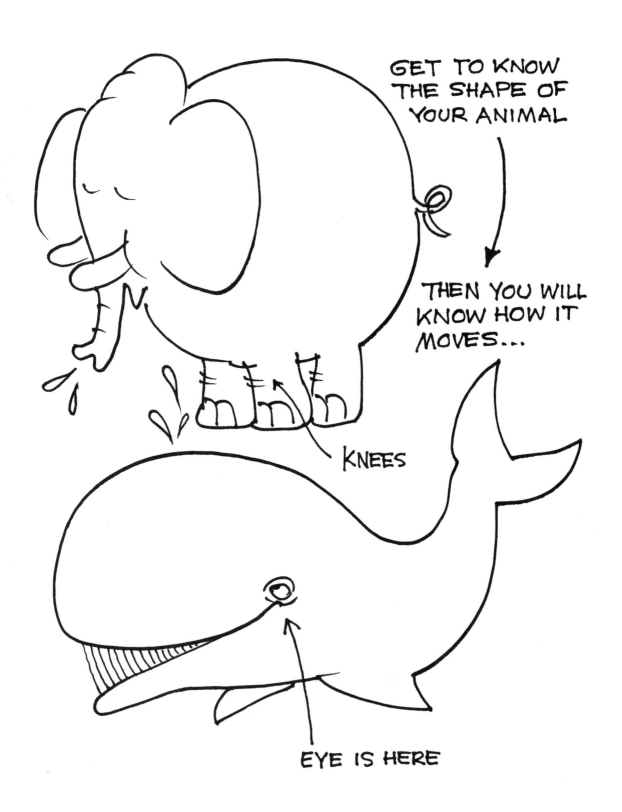

STICKING FACES ON A CIRCLE...

WITH A LITTLE THOUGHT AND IMAGINATION YOU CAN CREATE A LOT OF DIFFERENT CREATURES JUST BY PUTTING A BEAK OR A NOSE ON A CIRCLE...

DRAW SOME CIRCLES AND HAVE A GO YOURSELF...

CIRCLES

IF YOU'VE GOT ONE OF THOSE CIRCLE GUIDES — USE THAT!

MICKEY MOOSE!

GDAFFi DUCK!

★ MAKE UP YOUR OWN CHARACTERS — OR JUST MIX UP DIFFERENT ANIMALS TO GIVE YOU A SINGLE CHARACTER

BILLY THE KID!

THINK ABOUT THE ACTION...

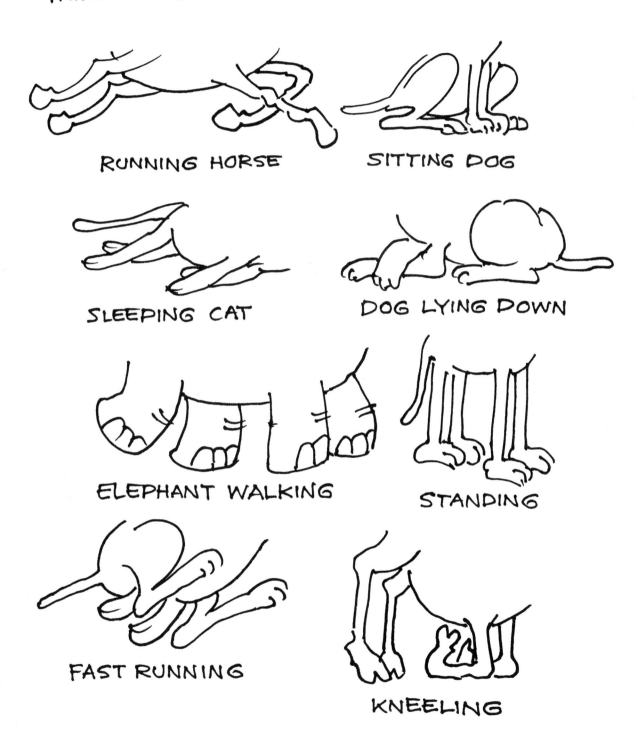

RUNNING HORSE

SITTING DOG

SLEEPING CAT

DOG LYING DOWN

ELEPHANT WALKING

STANDING

FAST RUNNING

KNEELING

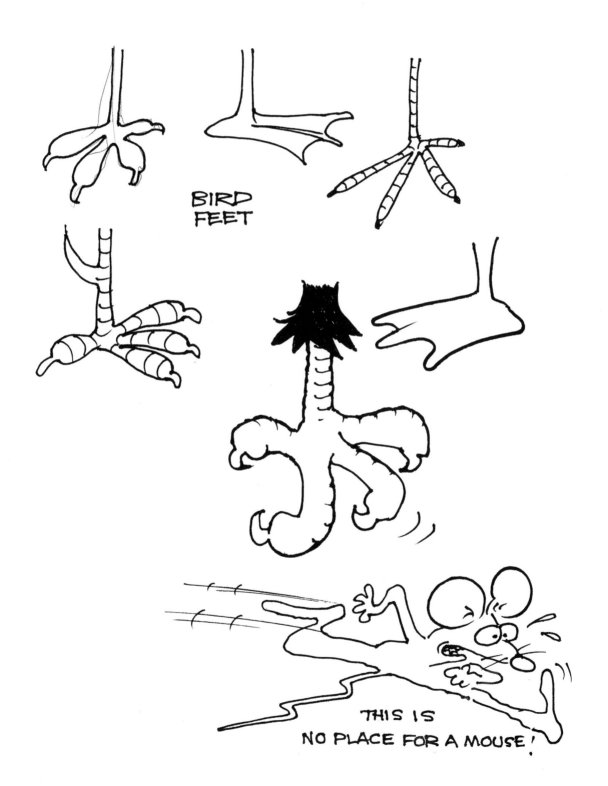

PUT THE HUMANS IN ANIMAL SITUATIONS...

MAKE THEM ——

MONSTERS

GIANTS ARE DRAWN FROM THE FEET UP TOWERING INTO THE SKY... SCARY STUFF!

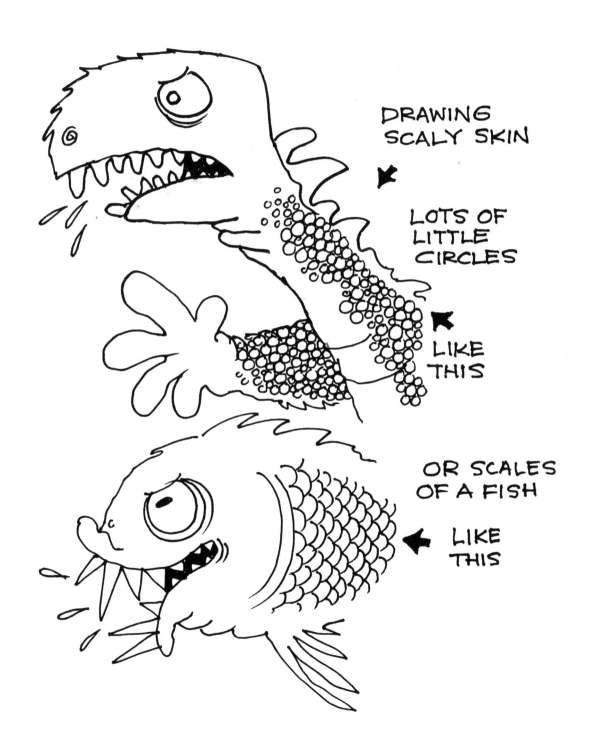

DRAWING
SCALY SKIN

LOTS OF
LITTLE
CIRCLES

LIKE
THIS

OR SCALES
OF A FISH

LIKE
THIS

— QUICKLY—THINK OF SOME MORE JOKES!

DRAWING CARTOON CARS AND BIKES...

DRAW A BOX WITH YOUR PENCIL

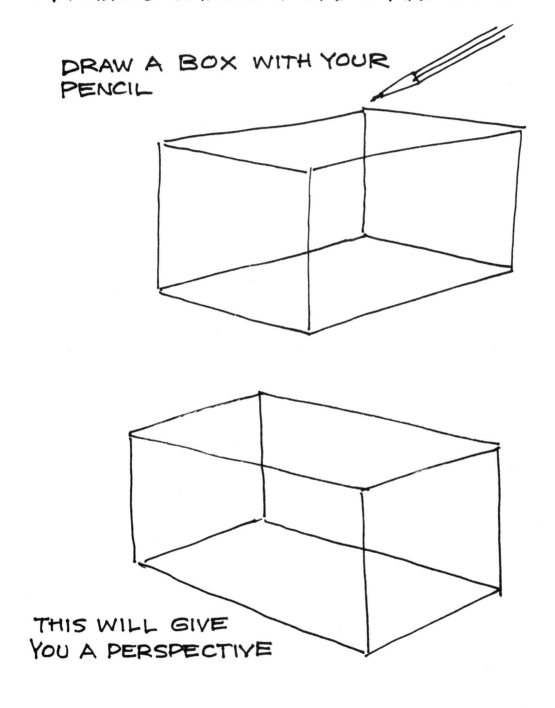

THIS WILL GIVE YOU A PERSPECTIVE

THEN DRAW YOUR CARTOON CAR
IN THE BOX...

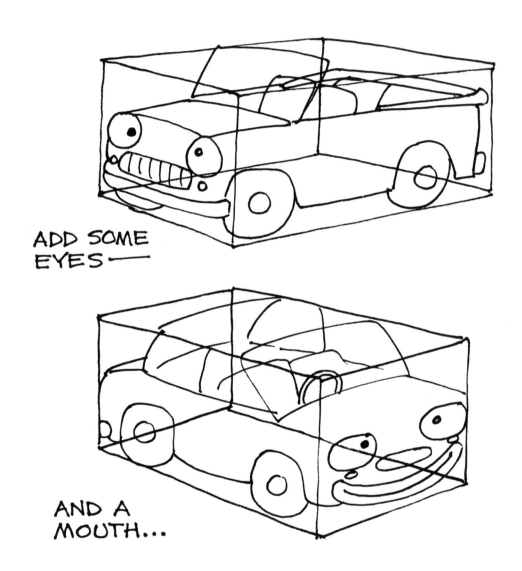

ADD SOME
EYES—

AND A
MOUTH...

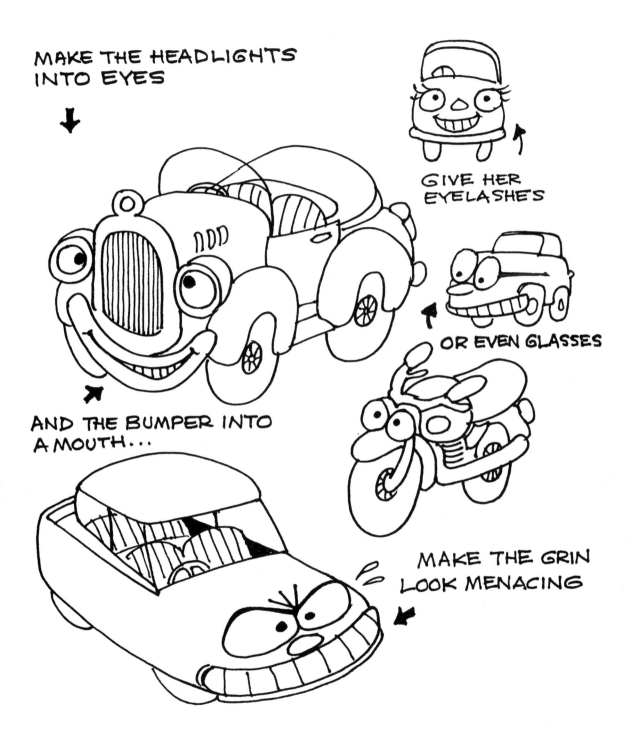

MAKE THE HEADLIGHTS INTO EYES

GIVE HER EYELASHES

AND THE BUMPER INTO A MOUTH...

OR EVEN GLASSES

MAKE THE GRIN LOOK MENACING

SKETCH OUT SOME PENCIL SHAPES...

THEN START TURNING THEM INTO
CARTOON PLANES WITH YOUR PEN —
GIVE THEM EYES AND A MOUTH WITH
LOTS OF DIFFERENT EXPRESSIONS...

CARTOON PLANES...

IF IT'S A PROPELLER PLANE
DRAW A CIRCLE WITH TWO
SQUIGGLES ➤

...AND DO THE SAME IF ➤
IT'S A HELICOPTER

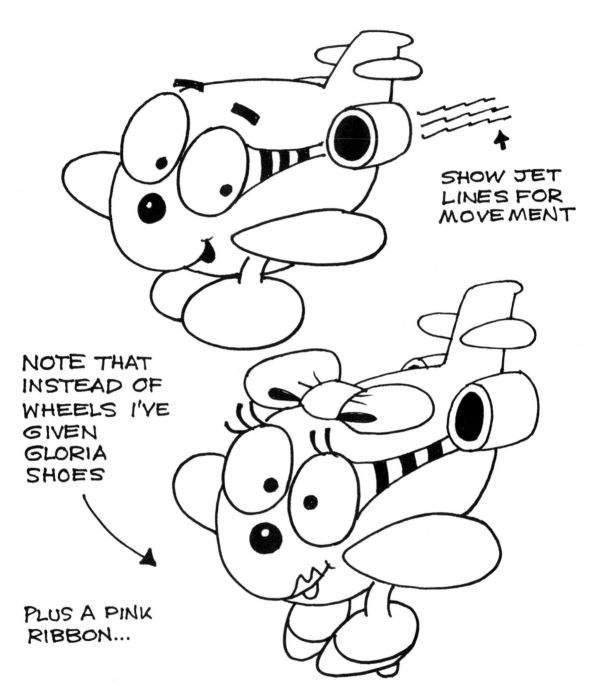

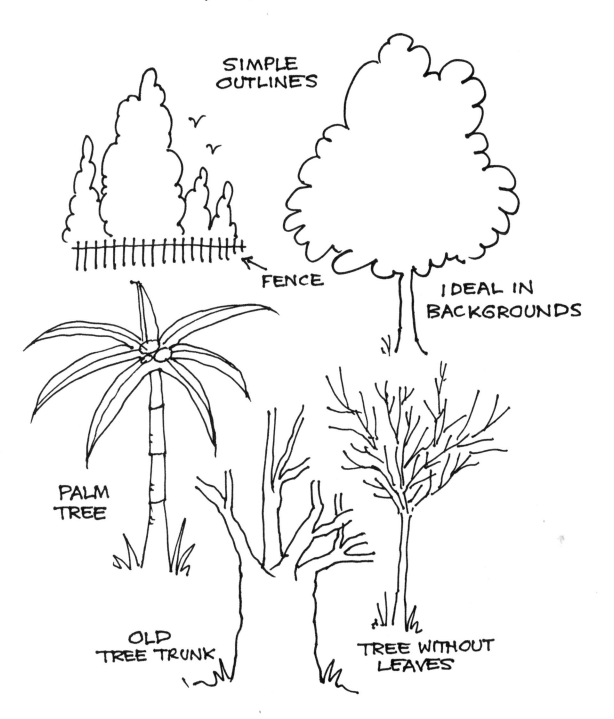

DRAWING TREES

SIMPLE
OUTLINES

FENCE

IDEAL IN
BACKGROUNDS

PALM
TREE

OLD
TREE TRUNK

TREE WITHOUT
LEAVES

MORE TREES...

A LITTLE
MORE DETAILED

TREES ARE IDEAL
FOR SETTING A SCENE

SIMPLE BRICKWORK:

OR ROOFING...

KEEP IT NICE AND OPEN...

DRAWING THE SEA
(DON'T FORGET THE SEAGULLS)

CARTOON PANELS

YOU CAN DRAW A STRIP CARTOON ANY SIZE YOU LIKE AND AS MANY PANELS — BUT USUALLY A STRIP CARTOON CONSISTS OF FOUR PANELS...

YOU CAN DRAW THEM ACROSS, DOWN OR IN A SQUARE...

IF YOU ARE GOING TO DO BALLOON LETTERING — KEEP IT NICE AND OPEN...

DON'T CRAM YOUR LETTERING INTO A SPEECH BALLOON!

YUK!

KEEP IT NICE AND OPEN!

EASY TO READ!

①

②

③

④

I HOPE THIS BOOK HAS INSPIRED
YOU TO TAKE UP THE PEN AND
DRAW CARTOONS...

HOWEVER, IF HAVING REACHED
THIS PAGE YOU FEEL IT'S ALL
BEYOND YOU — TURN TO MUSIC!